The Never

The Never

poems by

Judith Skillman

Dream Horse Press
California

Library of Congress Cataloging-in-Publication Data:

Skillman, Judith
        The Never
                p. 92   cm

                        ISBN 978-1-935716-00-6
                        1. Poetry

10 9 8 7 6 5 4 3 2 1

First Edition

Cover art: Josh Tuininga, Winter Birches, 2009. Pastel on board.
Cover design: Josh Tuininga

Contents

The Never

"…And bees
When, drunk on the scent
Of Spring, are stirred
By the spirit of the sun, driven
Erratic in its pursuit, but when
Burnt by a ray, they all veer back
Abuzz, filled with premonition…"

Friedrich Holderlin, Hymns and Fragments

for my family: Tom, Drew, & Jocelyn; Lisa & Josh Tuininga;
Klara June & Hazel Anne Tuininga

I. Quicksand

The Crinolines

In cages readied beside water,
in crab pots dropped from the rowboat
where an oar bleeds into an oarlock,
from land and water they come—
farthingale, petticoat, pannier.

If it is difficult to hold the umbrella steady
under rain that sheets,
think of the woman who enters the carriage
as if she were the first one
to wear the newfangled cloth of reform.

She stands, feet planted beneath
her shoulders as if she were ready
to take on the gods of satire
in a heady gust of wind.
The crinolines are burning, in lumber

piled beside a well-stocked
garage, in crinolettes and gadgetry
of the last century piled haphazardly
one on the other. In cotton
that smells of sweat and horses,

in nylon bearing the stain of blood.
The bride stands on her pedestal
wearing a bustle that has returned
for its chance to bear
the brunt of history.

Doppelganger

You there in the corner —
say a word or two.
Throw us something
to chew on, some grass
or a slender reed
we might blow on
until the tones rise
and enter our bones
like a Tibetan prayer bowl
rimmed by a bamboo stick.
Hey you two, members
of the clan of the unborn —
come here and answer
for what you've done.
What, mirror images?
One left-handed, one right?
One parochial, one secular?
It was the zygote split
you into clones. In June
the lilac rusts, blossom-heads
welded like Siamese twins.
June and the wild cherry
drops stems for lack of bees
to pollinate the sweets.
It's not enough
not to be annihilated
by a vision. Nor do we
wish to carry our bodies

forward against the blunt
weather told by a map
empty of all but symbols.
How could we envy what
we never had? Admit
that hunger will be your
demise. Grow infantile.
Slip from your mother
one at a time,
bound by a cord,
fed by the bloody
sun and moon
stuck in orbit
around one another.

The Chickens Don't Lay

We bring them plastic eggs,
we dog them with our need.

Cluck cluck's stuck
to the back of our throats,

we try to talk them down
from the rafters.

They've grown into the names
we gave them — *Helen and Iris* —

the one golden, the other striped
with colors that fatten by the day.

We built a house for them
out back, and daily we up their feed.

Virgin lumber and fresh hay
trigger desire. Maybe we'll wake

and find a nest with a swollen pearl in it.
We thought we wanted goats,

pigs, a donkey or mule,
but what we needed most

was for the cackling to die down to a whisper,
the whisper to silence.

Then to walk out along
stones we laid by hand,

a path to their coop
near cedars and elk.

To swaddle the delicacy
in hands weathered by water and cold,

we who paid too much for all we have,
and less than nothing for what went wrong.

The Last Pie Bird

A crusty fellow
ripe with juice and seeds.
A bit of *bling* shoved
beneath the crust.

Proof a secret prison might lie,
like a shunt, to wick steam.
The heat in its belly makes berries
burst like bombs—

the Marion, the blue, the raspberry.
Four and twenty blackbirds
come from the essence of sugar.
Betrayal killed the lyric, but the pie bird survived.

Its neck stretches into the kitchen
for air. Sing a bit, wee bird.
We've forgotten what a trinket means.
Teach us how to wrest sweetness from our days

when the second has been broken
down to a millisecond, the particle arrayed as quark and halo,
the genome come unbraided,
and Dolly-the-sheep cloned.

Pie bird, bard of Orpheus,
the river's gone black and berry-thick
with hell and how to get there.

The world can't bear to hear you sing
the single note that clots bloody stains baked into this
tablecloth, its blotch of history.

Darning Knob

Back when there were socks
to be mended, when a woman
thought to mend them,
she took this wand

and remembered her own feet—
cold, the little toe white and naked
in the snow.
When socks were hand-knit

the foot was important—
where it had been,
what it had walked through, and how.
Whether in summer or winter.

One way or another, in war or peacetime,
the thick tongues of shoes
had a way of coming apart
from their soles.

Others would come and go,
but these people were her own.
There were clothes to be washed,
wrung, hung out to dry.

A washbasin embossed
with porcelain flowers. A yard
where no one else could see
the threads of daylight.

Cobblestone Streets

Made for trouble,
meant to slow things down.
Narrow alleys,
lines of laundry to reel in,
a language smelling of garlic and gutturals.
Colors, scents, and secrets.
The street will not tell,
the map will not get you found.

These cars, these houses—
look now, none of them are yours.
Admit you are lost.
That you came from Europe
and can't remember when or why.
Perhaps there was a war.
A girl, barely a woman,
smiled at a man.

Skimpy clothes were thrown down,
right there, on the stones.
The moon was slim.
The earth was a flat plate, an offering
still full of fish and Tarsiers.
Someone had died of drink.
A pillar of stones for memory,
flowers piled in a cairn.

Flatiron

A woman with colorless hair
stands in a yard singed by summer.
Behind her the screen door, its broken hinge.

Her child's dressed in a balloon suit.
In the kitchen a basket full of damp linens.
The flatiron blackens, takes on heat.

How far away the child, who knows nothing
of his mother but voice, crochet hook, wash basin…
It's the iron has worn her down, hefting its weight to pillowcases,

wielding her triangle into corners of shirts vexed by stain.
Who can arson the past when its articles remain—
salt and pepper shakers, thimbles, kittens, scones.

The woman regards us from a yard age has yellowed.
Her man, underground with his canary,
will return punctually as dirt for supper.

On the porch that caricature of the child billowing like a parachute.
In her starched smile the story
of how he was wrenched from her by tongs.

Amphora

To be statuesque,
to bear the heady essence
of camphor oil,
or oil pressed from olives.

Not to be dropped
or used by fancy.
To be the bearer
and the mourner at once.

To bequeath
all that is not inscribed
in marble, the everyday
travail of citizens

sickened by the laundry
of their former selves,
those who were carefree
and shared bounty

in a house full
of adult laughter.
To bear what can't
be borne any longer

and rise under the strain
of patience—hands
as handles grasping the hysterical
one, the innocent

ensnared by her own body.
Unlimbering the grasp
of an infant who cannot let go
the spoon, the autistic one

tethered to home by thought,
the adult woman ill
with an illness deemed chronic,
her face become porcelain

as the visage of sun and moon.
To hold these qualities
in opposition and carry
them all lightly, without missing

a single step in the chain
of generations stretching
from Egypt to Greece to Rome
to Carthage to Spain.

After a dinner of skewered hens,
to hop-scotch Polynesian
islands, where exotic birds
wear their luxurious ruffles

to a breakfast of worms
proffered from the earth by rains.
Where whomever eats the eater

goes far beyond a repast of grubs,

continues toward the primitive feast
of fat, muscle, gristle, tendon,
bone. To peer down
into a tone-deaf odalisque

and see how altruism
on behalf of the one
equals sacrifice of the many,
if only for the sake of waging war.

Calling the Pigs

The scent's gone stale
and the memory's fetid
but he would stand
until it became important
that he be the only man
to care for pigs mired in mud.
Sooo-eee. Sooey sooey sooey sooooo-eeeee.

One by one they'd come,
furred and nimble, cloven-hoofed.
He had nothing to give them
so he pulled tendrils of grass
up by the roots
and fed it through wire.

Grasses were taken
into snout and stomach
and became more than the sum
of a life surrounded by women
who didn't understand
why he stood most nights
with his back to them,
his hat askew in the light
that spent itself in loss and gain.

The mud dried on his work shoes
and fell to the tiled floor
when he walked into the house

nights after calling the pigs.

It was these small cakes of dirt
Mother swept with her broom,
muttering under her breath,
beads of sweat
gathering on her forehead.
Then he sat back in the armchair
satisfied that the pigs had come,
the pigs had come to him.

Dengue

Thailand, 2004

With proboscis, compound eyes and net wings,
a hundred whirring machines
circled and landed on our skin.
Two young women in a two-man tent,
we zipped the screen, closed
cloth windows with metal snaps.

We shut the canvas door, pulled
sleeping bags up to our mouths
in ninety-degree heat. The ocean
crocheted saltwater,
foamed and frothed,
turned creatures into cretins.

How many hermit crabs
died that night?
We heard the sound of our own hands
swatting the tent wall,
accompanied by cussing
and hissing.

With every swat, each bad word,
the shock of blood
reddened dank walls.
At dawn we found swollen welts
on arms and necks,
beneath our thick, humid hair.

Breasts and thighs weren't spared.
On my ankle a red bruise
became a hellish itch.
We drove back to the bungalow
in a silence inclined toward insanity—
its fevers and hallucinations.

A Foreign Beer Garden

Wherever there were poor,
there were pelicans.

Laundry strung on lines in the rain.
I remember the scoop and swallow,

the smiles of a widow and her daughter
setting tables in an outdoor restaurant.

Later the chairs stood on their front legs in a warm rain,
the tablecloths were folded, their flowerings

bizarre as the hot pepper envelope
in which sheets of cheese melted.

I remembered being poor and hot,
hearing my Mother mention stone soup.

At night vivid imaginings.
Grasshoppers crossed my pillow, crickets sang

from embankments. Don't think the sea forgets
what it carries—a resemblance, a blank stare,

and then, once more, the waiter with one eye
standing before our table, asking about drinks.

Serum Sickness

By the time she sits down
it is already late,
well into the syrup-colored skies
of another autumn.
The leaf of basil she picked

to scent olive oil
almost overpowers her.
Chrysanthemums, purchased
as an afterthought with a bag of groceries,
have spindled out of hand.

Low brow grapes wince
as they creep, still green,
along their trellis—
a length of chain link
behind the convenience store.

To be watered on a whim
is the same as
being watered too much.
To be ogled, handled, squeezed—
it all amounts to a case of nerves.

She dawdles on the porch,
watches for the squirrel,
that prankster
who became her master last summer.
By the time her body realizes it's been had—

too many antibodies in the blood—
it's too late to take back
grimaces, words, and arguments
enhanced by low-grade fever.
She eyes the polish on her nails—

Nantucket Pink this week,
toned down like the season.
Still wet, glistening
like a syringe
with the gleam of overkill.

Hot and Cold

Lucretius knew
　　　　the middle ground
was all a man could see.

　　　　　　The extremes would make
a person go mad—
　　　　　　　hypothermia,
　　　　where the snow becomes
　　　　　　　a soft bed of down,
has claimed the best climbers.

In the heat
　　　　of a closed-up place
an old woman dies
　　　　　　from the same dream
　　　　that made life exciting
when she was young.

We are caught
　　　　off balance,
trying to right ourselves
　　　　when it snows in April.

Summer lasts
　　　　past late-October,
　　　　　　the rose puts out one more
Lincoln bloom.

We don't think to question
        the laziness in our heads,
                floaters rising and falling
like dance gnats
        in our retinas.

We know enough
        not to ask
for more than this world,
        its twinned blossoms
                of flower and snow—

its feverish kisses,
        powdered masks,
                whirling dervishes
and incestuous whims.

II. Land Bound

The Sister

First-born in every version
          of the story.
Even as a twin
she came first.

The hard pushes
          were for her.
She grew faster,
ate more and better,

turned over first,
          walked on quadriceps.
And yes, she was jealous.
Used her sibling as a crutch,

pushing the dark head down
          to raise herself
a notch higher.
They played in the grass

until the grab and shove
turned the younger sister,
the one born
          with its curse—

that once-mild child
chorused full-throated shrieks.
The cat ran,

the dog shied away

from Cain's pig-squeals
and fat, fur-laced fingers.
      Cain grew weedy.
She hid in the laurel hedge.

Her sharp nails,
like morning glory
blooms, spiraling
      chokeholds.

And those seeds—
      hallucinogenic—
she shook six into her palm
before choosing her weapon.

Death of Pan

We were only playing in the pasture,
wearing a patchwork of sun and sky,
ragged with the coming autumn.
That is to say we didn't mean
to drown out the sound of his flute—
our piper, nor meddle with the conch shell
that caused our fathers to panic.

And his Arcadia—
how we adored her. We made wreaths
of wildflowers, twined tendrils of her hair
around our stubby hands as we brought
her one more gift: a leaf bloodied with color,
a spare sapling, an agate choked in quartz.

       Until the river-god,
happy as ever to be plunged in cold,
took him from our arms and flung
his instrument against the rocky shore.
The syrinx shattered into seven reeds or nine,
and we, still infatuated with the echoes
our voices made in that valley, called out
to one another, not so much from loneliness
as the excitement of recitation.

         Light breezes
dog us as we go forward in reconnaissance,
teaching one another how to suffer

being schooled by lechers. Our appetite

for the one called *Pitys*—another nymph

loved by him, who turned into a pine tree

to escape his overtures,

runs nil to none.

Dodo Bird

with lines from Holderlin

I found it land-bound, small wings tucked
against its sides. The head naked,
almost human in its appraisal.
I remember hearing about you, I said
and it replied *For the gods grow indignant…*

It was not repulsive, rather oily, a few black strands
like leftover feathers sprouting from its head.
I thought you were a figment I said,
and it replied *if a man not gather himself to save His soul…*

I said I was a woman, that I would have preferred
to lose the ostrich, but would not starve my children.
If there had been a famine and the opportunity arose
I also would have beaten the Dodo to death
with whatever was at hand—
club, baseball bat, plank of wood,
but I wouldn't have laughed.

Women are tame.
We don't kill unless threatened.
Did you not perceive the Dutchmen as a threat?
Yet he has no choice…
the bird replied, foraging, head down,
diamond eyes shrunken to slits
as it pried grubs from mud.

Why have you grown so large—
three feet tall, walking about
as if you owned the ground
between clouds of idealism and germs of reality.
You had your heyday.
We have your beak in the British Museum
for proof: DNA, some writings and renderings.

It went about the business of the omnivorous—
scavenging, turning its *arse* this way and that,
always the silly walk of it
and the precious non-birdness of its serious demeanor,
unshaken by extinction: *like-*
wise; mourning is in error…

The Rat

Is back, scurrying
with the profile
of a Jew down
in back, which Céline
said, and he is dead,
which Dieudonné says
and he's alive.
The rat is back
all of a piece,
prophetic as dawn's
fallen rabbi, the dark
robe split down
the middle.
The cage empty,
the cities punctuated
rat tat tat,
by grenades that mine
the guts of land
and doctors who
wrench pellets of shot
from the belly.
The rat, an object
of desecration,
a perjury, a black lie,
an angel with the claws
and nose of a Jew.
How is it
the temple built

for three holds only
the one rat,
its offal, its fancy
arabesque of retreat
and overture,
an invitation
to partake in the feast
of pomegranate rice,
of duck fat gone white
as an eye that can
no longer see
what it came for.
The rat—how
many have written
it into oblivion
only to have it
pop back up
out of the sewer?
Bearing up under
our curses, rat
finds the jugular
while the thief
runs at a woman's
scream. Well-placed
in any story,
watchful, nimble
as a pet.
What we cherished

was, after all,
only the extinction
of the right species,
and, knowing
we got that wrong,
we tolerate the rat.

From the Grasslands

We came to an ocean paved with clouds.

Entered the remains of a forest.

Found strands of green coiled around rock.

The serpent lived here just as in the past.

We walked lightly, our shoes stained with meadows.

The quarter moon hung in daylight.

Iodine on a wound.

The sea boiled carbon dioxide stew.

Both manta ray and angel fish were gone.

An oasis changed from blue to a shade we did not know.

We stopped trying to drink bits of rainwater we'd collected
        on our tin roofs.

Ducts swollen shut from disuse.

The myths died and settled at our feet like elephant seals.

Our clothes wore more deeply than our dreams.

The sun came out of hiding to redden our skin.

It was then that the world caught fire.

Bending to Work in the Heat

Rows and columns,
the corn raising its silk tassels in august ceremony,
my mother tethered to her shovel,
breaking red Maryland clay
        into chunks.

Nothing single in that garden—
flies, and their cousins,
        the horseflies,
bees, and their sisters,
        the wasps.

The sun spawned
        a twin
    in milk-blue sky.
I remember what needed to be tended—
dirt, virgin zucchini and tomatoes.

        In pure solicitous warmth
the heat became our primer.
We absorbed its thirsts and irritations,
its longings. I stepped on a hornet.
My gloveless hands found worms
        halved by mother's shovel.

Maternal garden, garden
where Adam and Eve
        melted into one another,

their arms and legs tangled,
        vined like the morning glory.
Whatever the heat wanted it took.

The sun fell into the Potomac by degrees.
A moon rose, cold to the touch—
        pink quartz, exotic dessert.

We were tamped by father's anger,
quelled by punishments
like the earth in mother's garden.

Drip of a casement air conditioner
that whet more than cooled
the starts of smooth, white breasts
        hung on the bones of our chests.

Those Bleeding Hearts

Well, naturally
they would have to go before the others.
Not after the lion, chimpanzee, zebra, or giraffe.
Certainly not post-monkey
and dog gangs roaming the streets
of an exiled city.

You could go so far as to say
endangerment would be endemic
to a species whose heart was located
by a red mark suspiciously like blood,
or by the sort of folk
who are overly sympathetic to lost causes—
those island birds, liberals, and ground doves.

They would have to be killed off.
If not by the exact spot
at which to take aim with a shotgun,
then by their own inbred ability
to ooze sap, juice, and pink heart-shaped flowers.
Their pilfering predicated on a tendency
to fall victim to extortion.
To be trimmed, to run together, to seep through
the covers, as in, stain.

Even to feel grief, pain, or other
equally splashy stubs of emotion
that might be later expanded upon

follows too closely upon the heels
of another animal—sentimentality.

What about the vivid red color
splashed across white breasts?
This is no time to wax precious
about their alleged disappearance.
We have heard rumors of sightings.

These bits of gossip and bleeps
have not been recorded with any certainty.
Who would want to give away
the location of that which lies outside the margin,
in the peaceable kingdom beyond pastoral boundaries.

Extinction's Cousin

I came back for scraps—
    what else could I carry in my dislocated jaw?

With my tough, oily flesh,
    what chance would I have of finding relatives?

I came for a theory.

    String theory, combustion theory.
        A shred of evidence:
"So, in an unsettling Damien Hirst-like tableau, the bird was
        beak to beak with its own face…"

I knew allusions would be required.

    Illegible notes,
        the certain rustling of papers
        unearthed as the dead make peace with the living,

that I must wait a considerable length of time,
as after a bereavement.

It has been that long.

    Here I stand before you wearing just plain skin.

What name will you give me,

the one without fur, scales, or feather?
What will you say to a second extinction?

I came to the island of trash, Mauritius,
near Madagascar, where there are certain butterflies
and jewels left among corrugated roofs and contraptions
to siphon rainwater into buckets that reek with odorous sulphurs.

I was looking for a fluke.

Perhaps the Dodo bird.

Give me something endemic to the landscape—

no palms, no sugarcane.

Allow me a shell, a bit of coral with some color left in it.

Can we name those we never knew?

Of the fragmentary Oxford Dodo, shopworn
and foul-smelling,

only articles from *Nature*
and DNA survive.

Let's sift through the passenger pigeon's leavings,
its calling cards and mother-of-pearl wings.

Are these our relatives?

    What do they say
        when they gather together
           for feasting?

What say when breaking a crust of rock to aid the search
        of a revered specialist, a man
who has traveled beyond tourism
        and hard candy
           to satisfy his eccentric needs for pelican teeth.

How will we deal with fossilized pollen?

    How excavate shit, mine mud, dig out

              glacial till to find a bone.

I came back for this—
"a great fowle somewhat bigger than the largest Turky cock."

    I came to the circus to see
        one Dodo who had survived its water passage
           to the British Isles.

The absurdly large bill frightened me into silence.

Wheatlands

To travel is to dream of wheat,
passing over and under the drape
and pleat of hill and valley, darts taken in
when floodwaters passed over the earth.

To dream is to revel in scenery,
to be nourished by land—its crop tarnished
by harvest, like the stubble on a man's face
that makes the face handsome to a woman.

To sleep is to travel inside the germ
and the chaff. To wake is to breathe
a fine dust rising, bedeviled.

To dream is to become the whirling dervish
stuck inside the golden hen—
that one—who clucked at us
about hysteria until the day she died.

Our journey takes a year, a week, a day,
or an hour. Roads the color of wood smoke
cross fields. A water table lies thirty feet down,
under soil thicker than flourless cake.

In drought, dun-colored pyramids
grow from the mouths of machinery.
Sun beats down on the Palouse.

We come to savor this crop grown brighter
than noon, poorer than dusk.
A whole hell full of dollars gone blank as a page.

We comb the fields with our eyes,
picking out threads of silence,
choosing the nap and the grain.
Prefer gold, the land says, and we do.

Picking Blueberries

Impressionistic, the poplars waving
above Mercer slough
where two boys hunt for snakes
using only a bucket and the machismo
they were born with.

The bushes tall and orange-red,
the berry stems like wicks
set to tease out blues from the furrows—
rows swollen and rubbed raw
by other pickers.

We like to take the easy ones
full of sweetness, like the painter who sees
nothing but paradisiacal imaginings
above his easel: couples in canoes,
couples in kayaks,

the paddle raised high
before it dips into water
to disturb a crust of algae.
The painter over his head
in beauty, entranced.

September. Another winter
quivers in the bog
as it moves toward us.
There we'll reinvent

dreams of summer.

Then we'll remember
the inky harvest—
whatever fell into our creased palms
to purple our fingers
and darken our tongues.

Parenthood

Here they come,
cretins scrawled one beside the other
in the dark. Indigenous
to themselves and each other,
here they come fastened together,
male and female like before.
He of the grunts and guffaws,
she of the quick laughter,
come all this way
from the Old Country,
which changed each time as soon
as it became a name.
Not that they wished to impose
on us, not in order
to please, certainly not to complain.
Flattened and scattered,
the stories helter skelter
and clothes on the floor,
it happens. What's in our blood,
twinned? What thins
the courage they've taken
from us simply by visiting?
It could be they're not out to displace us,
only want to find a trick
they left behind, whether
it had a heart or not,
how many legs did it have,
and was it going to love them
no matter what or how sadly
they became.

Rag and Bones Man

Not so much scavenger as savior—
balloons tied to his horse's harness
to tempt the children out
of the poorhouse.

> *Et begun ike ve crows, who,*
> *seein' the gleam of a fing might be*
> *human—*
> *button,*
> *remnant,*
> *bet uv metool hoop*
> *slipped from a girl's skirt*
>
> *that gleam fredding sod...*

Out of the shanty of leftovers, heels, and table scraps
the young ones came running, wearing
remnants of rags,
second, third-hand hand me downs.

> *I begn tah do et—seein as de casual*
> *founderer*
> *'as his own value,*
> *be it measured in glue, iron, fabric, paper...*

Who gets up when the missus' milk's gone dry?
Who wrests the worm from the robin
and the grub from the dirge

of the woodpecker?

Me eyes n'ands knew enuf to make a nest for me own children.

Nothing to weep for—
he wasn't a household man.
He didn't mind boarding a bus
carrying stuff to sell elsewhere.

Et wa'nt a fing could spike me 'abit

Came the automobile
and the waste pickers were out of work,
even the dung beetle, that most pure consumer,
that litter monger.

Traded me horse for a lorry…

Still the calls came by telephone: fridge,
scarred Corrado parts,
washbasin, jug,
claw foot tub holding weeds and offal.

T'wa'n't more different than a raven feeding on a small dead shark—

He wasn't as rare as the customs collector,
not as rude as the inspector
though he could hold his own

against the maw of cold.

> *I got th' coppers,*
> *they lind me pockets*
> *like the mother-o' pearl fools*
> *those swine*
> *drunk agin*
> *& snortin' their own piss —*

It must have been a wet month in the hundred-year war
when he disappeared with the symbols
of the costermongers: horseshoe,
dove, heart, cross, flower pot.

> *But down curss me mum,*
> *down sew me into yr bk of baryin' beetles, blowflies, yellerjackets, r'ccoons.*

Gone like the pearly kings and queens,
with no return address
but progress, the trick that grinds
its own filthy wheel.

III. The Grounds of Heaven

Picasso's Toad

Two days into autumn
and the saws begin to saw,
the beds to moan with lovers
parked beneath quilts
as if under tea cozies.

Two days into fall and wood smoke
drifts through a window
stripped of its screen, tar
from a neighbor's burn barrel
coughs and settles.

How long has it been?
I wanted you. Once
upon a time we foraged
hands and mouth beneath
the brocade spread.

Better not to state the obvious—
the seven-year itch come and gone
so many times my arms
sprout hives, my scalp's on fire.
Seborrhea, the doctor said,

and wrote out a prescription
with an inkless pen
on his Blackberry. *Let it
begin with me*, I think, a slogan,
but still...

All the way to the pharmacy
I carried the image—
a newsprint study
hung in a gallery
housed in a mall.

There was nothing loathsome
about the creature
who hunched over hollow reeds
as if it had come
to taunt us with quicksand.

Who will dare to tell the truth
about the end of passion?
Who will state the obvious
about the ornate life—
its gaudy curlicues and frenzied paisleys.

Accretion

It begins in the back yard.
A light blanket of petal snow
coats the patio table,
pinks the earth as it warms to sun.

We wonder whether
we were lost to one another
all winter, and how did one thing
add to another until our speech

became slurred and we muttered
curses under our breath,
certain no one would hear.
Not our loved ones, not God,

nor the Saints in their plainclothes
roaming the grounds of heaven.
We wonder how life started,
though we know it began

to snow without the violence
and the cold. Perhaps we remember
watching a different kind of weather
drift more slowly

than we thought possible,
passing in the wind, the windows
dirtied with storms and bird droppings,
the breeze carrying scents

of blood and birthing.
We stand beside our own bodies
and notice we have free will.
So the devil's not been banished.

Yesterday you counted a hundred
cysts on the plum tree.
Blueberry-shaped blossoms
suffer in order to become *bluets*

on the bush. Tiny oranges
erupt, blanched from *leaf curl*
on the nectarine. Pie cherries
follow newborn crows.

If the devil's been let into the kingdom
to do his bit—the *I would be happy but for x . . .*
still, at dawn or dusk,
this odd snow adds a tinge of cobalt

to the pale shell of quarter moon.
Its dark side tipped toward us
as if to soak up the last third
of our lives, which is the best.

Field Mouse

It was found in Spring prunings,
left to rot by the cat.
Lifted gingerly by its tail,
and the woman who put it in a paper bag
felt the shiver of flesh
before she smelled the scent of carrion.

This was not unlike other days
spent putting on blush and powder
in the suburbs.

Perhaps the woman realized—
in her kinship with the dead,
in her love of cats and the petted life—
how much she had in common
with other creatures.

Shrews. Goblins.
She was soft, that woman, and small-boned.
How to say the truth without scolding?
How sally forth into the world
without a snout and a temper?

Quaking Aspen

for Jack Gilbert

It was the least breeze
that brought you to me—
or was it gray-green leaves
turning over to show
how white they were,
paper-white.

The flattened leafstalks
made it easy
to change our minds.

Old Poet, I see you
fluttering, trembling
where you stand,
finally attached to a woman.
Fame wasn't interesting,
you said.

It's her children,
the girl and boy
you never had,
the ritual of the dinner table
that keeps you
at her side.

Fancy or imagination—

you left me with a conflict
worse than any fiction.

Old Poet, remember we ate Thai food
and looked across the water
where Charon had just finished
ferrying Michiko
across to Hades.

Later she would
return in poems,
in the shrine
on your dresser,
each time a petal dropped
from a flower.

I am still married
though I have strayed,
and not for you. Fancy
or imagination?
The fabric of leaves,
many-storied, makes room
for alibi's.

I see the aspen and want
to place a streetlamp
and a trollop beside it.

Nothing perennial
except sleep and dreams.
Nothing temporal
but the way you molded
your body to mine
when I said
I would be going.

Another Ice Age

Grasshoppers fly from rocks
to roots to moss
to goats beard.
Queen Anne's lace
opens its snowy doilies.
Bees make a heavy frieze
of Scotch Broom.
I wander farther
than the master ordered.
I grow sick with thoughts
of the homeland.
I pine for the highest
province—altitude,
the desert country
that never loved me back.
And when I stare down
at fire ants, I see
their segmented bodies—
half black, half red—
teeming thousands
who rush from nest
to warfare like Lilliputian
soldiers. They cross twigs
and bent flowers
as though the works
of aggression could stopper
the brutal animal of ice,
that changeling who lives
off the crust of the earth.

Palm

Do you remember we sat beside
  sand and water, listened
as coconuts fell, one per minute?

They landed so close
  to our bistro table
we joked about prisoner's heads.

They say if you are before a firing squad
  you ask for a cigarette—
    not for a meal, not for a drink.

So many heads, one per minute,
    hitting the sand
      with the sound of proscription.

    Heads from every country,
landing close to our meal of prawns,
    chicken, rice, and beans.

    We can have whatever we like
      in this version of paradise.
    We can make love long and slow
under a white sheet

      and then walk down
    to listen to the tide
folding itself onto the beach

in a perfect funnel, only to rush back
where it belongs,
in the belly of the bay
that opened with a fissure
four years ago
and took the sand.

We can stay here,
where coconuts fall
like the light-lidded heads
of men before a firing squad,
heavy heads of men
who were hung or guillotined
or worse.

The palm keeps
climbing upward,
its gnarled bark like the skin of the old.

If those sharp leaves—
the ones that make steep roofs
for the palapas—

have any doubts about
keeping off the rain,
they only feather the sky
with light
as if to make it tremble.

The Never

They lie in separate rooms while the moon
spills its light across limbs of trees.
The fake owl poses in the yard next door—
those yellow eyes she saw and thought
it was a Great Horned Owl. The *never*
comes in spurts, like wings across the kitchen
skylight cutting her off from him
during the day. *Never* takes the form of sleep
at night. It's not that *never* belongs
to no one else. Practically anyone
could be happy under the sentence of moon
on gravel, moon on frost, moonlight
on fake owl perched in a willow.
Perhaps the moon is birch wood, she thinks,
and it was part of the *never* before this *never*.
Maybe the wings are obsidian and covered
the skylight when a piece of the Kuiper Belt
exploded above their house. Inside she feels
a bit like *never*. Likes the sound of mingling
with folks that might live there. Likes the fake owl,
who never asks *who*.

An Invitation

Come inside where it's warm
and I'll take off your past
like a jacket. Come sit by the fire
and feel for the last five-dollar bill
in your pocket. Watch it curl and burn,
lend a bit of turquoise to color
        the flame.

Come in from the woods,
from the paper mill, the sumptuous odor
of whatever it is you've been making
along with atrocity. You must know
I have been waiting for your arrival.
You must feel the stain of my hand
on your arm, see the bit of beard I've grown,
despite my being, or having been,
        a woman.

Come inside. There are potatoes
with poisonous eyes and apples gone soft
at the middle. I've seen what you do
with your life and I forgive you. I've met
the middleman and forgiven him. When
you and I go together to meet whomever
is waiting for us—can you hear
the saxophone wailing, the little train
        without a caboose…

When we find ourselves at the end
it will be in the rain or beside the sea.
When we're gone, the same dull rain
will fill an impartial sea. Only our feet
will be cold, the gray leather soles of us
like two stiffs out for a night on the town,
naked except for

       our blue toes.

Blue Agate

See how it rounds
out the rock
like a jewel,
a sapphire
taken from the mines.

Only a wish,
a sparkle of mica,
the hope of a counterfeit
gem, this stone
kept in body of the earth

until it could
no longer pretend
that time would allow
it to become
what it would never be...

And yet, the color, that color—
where ice and cornflower
stand and wait
for the meeting
of sky and water.

The Rumble Seat

Not that I mind riding
these stories of the past,
bumping along into the country
with the cousins and uncles,
a bit of dirt kicked up
to lather my face…

Not that I mind hearing
the same stories over
and again, their nuance
finally clear as the streams
where they first festered
and began to own their lives
as we cannot…

Do me a favor, you
up there in the front,
go on driving slowly
past cows whose udders
sweep the grass,
willows and cypresses
the color of sun on rust…

Keep talking while I rest
a little longer
at the beginning of industry,
where the milk has its head
of cream and comes in green

glass, where the newspaper
riffles its own pages
in the wind…

Let my mother
be young again, courted
by men who want to take her
away from my father,
who has become strong
in his new body taken
from the guts of an engine…

Feeder

How many secrets
were bequeathed to the earth
by its needle-beak—
that *poseur*, the hummingbird,
playing at a feeder
of sweetened water
a widow placed before her window
even after the wild currant
had bloomed.

Epilogue

Rain all day off and on
and to be stuck in a cottage
by the sea, a path leading down
to the lighthouse, a path leading up
to the site of fortresses
graffiti'd now, roofs open to sky,
sheaves of goats beard
slung down into the battery
where cannons were stored.
In one photo of WWI, a practice drill,
men hold their ears as the cannon
goes off. In another, officers
form a makeshift band —
trumpets and French horns,
the piano behind, its bench empty.
A player piano? Who knows how long
between the death-prick and the death,
or how Rilke handled suffering
since his soul suffered so upon being born.
What angel hovered beside him
when they put the leeches on him?
What was her name? Her province —
comfort or pain? I used to think
his verses precious, but that might
have been just a bad translation.
How does it happen that a man
named for a woman, a man who writes
elegies and sonnets that foretell nature's

dominion over man, can suicide
of having been infected by a rose?
His was this other, made-up garden
of Orpheus and Eurydice—half-gods
who nourished him until he died
from the injection of pure beauty.

Notes

"The Chickens Don't Lay" is dedicated to Lisa and Josh Tuininga.

"Amphora" was inspired by the exhibit "Roman Art from the Louvre" at the Seattle Art Museum, 2008.

"Dengue" was written for Drew Skillman, who journeyed to Thailand in October, 2004 and returned six days prior to the Christmas day tsunami.

In the poem "The Death of Pan," the word *syrinx* refers to an archaic hand-made flute.

In "The Dodo Bird," lines quoted from Friedrich Holderlin are taken from "Hymns," *Hymns and Fragments*, Princeton University Press, Princeton NJ © 1984.

The assertion by Céline in "The Rat" is taken from Louis-Ferdinand Céline, *North*. Translated by Ralph Manheim. Dalkey Archive Press, ©1996.

Quoted passages in "Extinction's Cousin" are taken from an essay by Ian Parker, *The New Yorker*, January 22, 2007.

Thanks to Jocelyn A. Skillman for her assistance with cockney dialect in "Rag and Bones Man."

"The Palm" was written after a trip to Mismaloya in Jalisco, Mexico.

"Blue Agate" refers to the agate digs on Red Top Mountain, near Ellensburg, Washington.

Acknowledgements

Thanks to the following journals, where these poems first appeared:

"The Crinolines," *Gargoyle, Verse Daily*

"Doppelganger," *Melusine*

"The Chickens Don't Lay," *The Broken Plate*

"Calling the Pigs," *Poesia*

"Darning Knob," *Miller's Pond*

"Field Mouse," *Roadkill Zen*

"The Last Pie Bird," *The Stickman Review*

"The Sister," *Seneca Review*

"From the Grasslands," *Midwest Quarterly*

"*The Never*," "Hot and Cold," *FIELD*

"Extinction's Cousin," "Parenthood," *The Fossil Record*

"The Dodo Bird," "Those Bleeding Hearts," "Picking Blueberries," *Tattoo Highway*

"Dengue," "Serum Sickness," *JAMA (Journal of the American Medical Association)*

"Wheatlands," "Another Ice Age," "Blue Agate," *The Northern Agrarian Review*

"Picasso's Toad," "Flatiron," *Inertia Magazine*

"The Rat," *The Poetry Revolt*

"The Death of Pan," "Rag and Bones Man," "The Rumble Seat," *Best Poem, Word Press*

"Quaking Aspen," *Poesia*

"The Crinolines," "The Last Pie Bird," and "From the Grasslands" were featured in the *2008 Jack Straw Writers Anthology*.

"Amphora" appeared in the anthology *Poets from Britain and America*, White Leaf Press, 2009.

"Cobblestone Streets" also appeared in *Heat Lightning, New and Selected Poems 1986-2006*, Silverfish Review Press.

Special thanks to my mother, Dr. Bernice Bloom Kastner, for her unstinting encouragement and support.

To Jack Gilbert, who never sought anything that didn't come his way.

I am indebted to my writer's group "The Young Poets"—Susan Lane, Joannie Kervran Stangeland, Anne Pitkin, and Darby Ringer.

Thanks to the Centrum Foundation for a residency at Fort Worden, where some of these poems were written.

About the Author

Judith Skillman's collection, *Heat Lightning: New and Selected Poems 1986 – 2006* was published by Silverfish Review Press. The recipient of an award from the Academy of American Poets for her book *Storm* (Blue Begonia Press, 1998), she has also received a King County Arts Commission (KCAC) Publication Prize, a KCAC Public Arts grant, and Washington State Arts Commission Writer's Fellowship.

Skillman's poems have appeared in *Poetry, FIELD, The Southern Review, JAMA (Journal of the American Medical Association), The Iowa Review, The Midwest Quarterly, Northwest Review, Seneca Review,* and numerous other journals and anthologies. She has been a frequent Writer in Residence at the Centrum Foundation in Port Townsend, WA. She holds an M.A. in English Literature from the University of Maryland, and has done graduate work in Comparative Literature and Translation Studies at the University of Washington.

A writer, editor, and educator, Judith lives in Kennydale, Washington with her husband. She enjoys the occasional company of her three grown children and fraternal twin grand-girls. Please see www.judithskillman.com for more information.

Other Titles by Judith Skillman:

"Prisoner of the Swifts," *Ahadada Books,* 2009

"Anne Marie Derése in Translation & The Green Parrot," *Ahadada Books,* 2008

"Heat Lightning: New and Selected Poems 1986 – 2006," *Silverfish Review Press,* 2006

"Coppelia, Certain Digressions" *David Robert Books,* 2006

"Opalescence," *David Robert Books,* 2005

"Latticework," *David Robert Books,* 2004

"Circe's Island," *Silverfish Review Press,* 2003

"Red Town," *Silverfish Review Press,* 2001

"Sweetbrier," *Blue Begonia Working Signs Series,* 2001

"Storm," *Blue Begonia Press,* 1998

"Beethoven and the Birds," *Blue Begonia Press,* 1996

"Worship of the Visible Spectrum," *Breitenbush Books,* 1988

www.ingramcontent.com/pod-product-compliance
Lightning Source LLC
Chambersburg PA
CBHW022030090426
42739CB00006BA/360